Dogs

by Michèle Dufresne

Pioneer Valley Educational Press, Inc

Here is a dog.
The dog is little.

This is a Pomeranian. This small dog usually weighs between 3 and 7 pounds. They make superb watchdogs and are great companions.

Here is a dog.
The dog is big.

This is a Newfoundland. They are known for their sweet nature, loyalty, and ability to rescue people in the water. They can weigh between 100 and 220 pounds.

Look at the big dog.
Look at the little dog.

The large dog is a Great Dane. This dog is known
for its giant size and its gentle personality. The puppy
is a Labrador Retriever. The Labrador is a popular
dog that can be very dependable, obedient, and fun.

Look at the dogs.
The dogs are little.

Here are Bella and Rosie. They are Bichon Frises, which means "curly lap dog" in French. Bichons are very intelligent and happy dogs. Their curly, white fur does not shed.

Here is a dog.
The dog is big and black.

This black dog is a Labrador Retriever.
Labradors come in different colors: brown,
black, and yellow.

Here is a dog.
The dog is little and brown.

This is a Chihuahua. Chihuahuas are the smallest dogs. They can be short- or long-haired. They have a curious nature. Like all dogs, they sometimes bite when frightened.

Look at the dogs!

There are many kinds of dogs. Some dogs are "pure breeds" and other dogs are a mix of several kinds of dogs.

Sheltie

Spaniel

Husky

Mixed Breed

Dalmation

Dogs

big

little

black

brown